THE BLUENESS OF THE EVENING

the blueness of the evening

SELECTED POEMS OF

HASSAN NAJMI

TRANSLATED BY
MBAREK SRYFI AND ERIC SELLIN

The University of Arkansas Press
Fayetteville
2018

ISBN: 978-1-68226-050-0
eISBN: 978-1-61075-627-3

22 21 20 19 18   5 4 3 2 1

Designed by Liz Lester

♾ The paper used in this publication meets the minimum requirements
of the American National Standard for Permanence of Paper
for Printed Library Materials Z39.48–1984.

Library of Congress Control Number: 2017947018

CONTENTS

III ▪ From *Seclusion*

IV ▪ *Umber Winds*

V ▪ From *A Hurt like Love*

PREFACE

I held the bottle to my mouth. I was trying to muffle
my scream. At a remote beach I threw it in the ris-
ing water. . . . I know that pearl divers in a faraway
gulf will hear my scream.

— HASSAN NAJMI, "Message in a Bottle"

The prestigious position that prose fiction and free verse have
been accorded in the Western literary tradition over the past
seven hundred years has only recently been mirrored in Arabic
literature. With the exception of the Holy Qur'an, which has
long held a privileged and inimitable place in the canon, the
Middle and Near Eastern literary tradition especially valued
ornate and highly structured verse and considered other creative
verbal expression, including widely appreciated tales like those
of *A Thousand and One Nights* and *Kalila and Dimna*, to be
less worthy. It was only in the mid-nineteenth century—which
marked an increase in the intellectual and artistic mediation and
exchange between European and Middle Eastern writing—that
the experimental tenets of post-classical European modernism
began to have a major impact on authors in the Arab world. It
should come, then, as no surprise that much of Moroccan liter-
ature today, whether in French, Arabic, or Berber, is still essen-
tially composed around an armature derived from the oral and
storytelling tradition of the area. For example, one can detect
indelible traces of that heritage in many recent Moroccan prose
works in the magical-realist vein, novels which tend to tell a

story until it has run its natural narrative course only to then conjure up another tale—sending in the clowns, so to speak (or, as in one of Tahar Ben Jelloun's novels, a troupe of acrobats from Marrakesh). There is also a predilection for episodic formatting and an oneiric aura created with suggestive nuggets that inspire the reader to invest more time and effort in the work—much as the listeners in the *halqa* circled around the storyteller at the Jemaa el Fna will drop coins or even tidbits of food into the narrator's hat or basket in order to learn the details of what will happen next, even if they are already familiar with the tale's general plot and outcome.

The long-standing preference for the episodic, the fantastic, and the enigmatic continues to this day in Moroccan literature. Short stories are quite popular, and contemporary novels in French or Arabic tend to be short and pithy or, if longer, are broken up into shorter episodes. Also, the growing acceptance of free verse as opposed to sometimes lengthy and highly intricate metrical structures has spawned an emerging school of poetry that draws energy from the narrative tradition of *A Thousand and One Nights*, the poems of Al-Mutanabbi, and the like, even as it finds inspiration in the immediate givens of the individual's cognitive world and takes structural and imagistic guidance from poetic role models like the Syrian Lebanese poet Adonis and various European and South American poets like André Breton, Paul Éluard, C. P. Cavafy, and Jorge Luis Borges.

Hassan Najmi's poems—with a few exceptions like "The Desert," a haunting rhapsodic elegy about friendship, loyalty, and mortality in the vast wastes of the Sahara—tend to be brief texts in free verse marked by dark and silent spaces that evoke a pervasive sense of absence and isolation of the sort found in the slightly ominous paintings of Edward Hopper or Vilhelm Hammershøi. Common are stark images of figures standing or sitting in almost palpable alienation among the familiar objects of an urban or domestic environment like a forlorn night café or a sparsely furnished residential interior. Najmi's minimalist poems, like these paintings, often seize and dissect mundane

moments of existence tinged with an obscure sense of deso-
lation, loss, failure, and longing. Consider, for example, the
unstated dramatic potential between the matter-of-fact lines of
"The Letters of Death":

> No water flowed under the bridge.
> Heads straightened on shoulders.
> The café is closed this morning, which is unusual.
> The bakery is empty.
> The bartender is drinking alone.

Najmi's shorter poems are often deceptively understated and
elusive and, like the Japanese haiku, demand the appreciative
reader bring to bear upon them a lingering inspection of the
sparse notes and the sympathetic vibrations or the dissonant
overtones that these superficially dissociated and sometimes
banal lines cause to resonate in the aerated spaces of the poem's
margins.

Hassan Najmi's poetry is not limited to introspective mus-
ings and existential speculations about the phenomenology
of his private world. He is also engaged in today's social and
political reality. Among the references to his cognitive envi-
ronment we occasionally encounter intimations of the polit-
ical oppression of the *années de plomb* ("years of lead"); and the
evanescent vignettes translated here as *Umber Winds* become
more comprehensible and compelling if we consider their gen-
esis. Najmi's poems in Arabic—accompanied by Abderrahman
Tenkoul's French versions and illustrated with black-and-white
ink washes by Moroccan artist Mohamed Kacimi (1942–2003)—
were published as *al-riyah al-buniyah* [الرياح البنية] / *Les vents
ochres* by Editions Marsam (Rabat, 2005). Najmi's poems and
Kacimi's washes were conceived independently in the early
1990s in response to the Persian Gulf War (an action sanctioned
by the United Nations but waged mainly by the United States)
and in particular to the massive aerial bombardment of Baghdad
in January and February 1991. Many Moroccan writers, though

no friends of Saddam Hussein's regime, found themselves conflicted by this international incursion into a sovereign Arab state and were horrified by the destruction of the civilian infrastructure and the heavy loss of life. Najmi and Kacimi learned of each other's creative responses to those events and decided to collaborate on this joint project. Their pictures and words memorializing the blasted lives and the destroyed dams, bridges, and homes in and around Baghdad are impressionistic abstractions but are clearly marked by political engagement and protest:

> Who will keep company with the orphaned glass
> when all the drunks have headed for the bridges of death?

> On their chests
> tons of explosives shall awake!

Hassan Najmi, like other Maghrebi writers, is performing at the intersection of *two* sets of cultural axes. He is on the one hand a product of the age-old cultural effervescence at the *geographical intersect* of the axis of East-West Arab-Islamic conquest, migration, and settlement and the North-South axis of contact, conflict, and colonial assimilation between Africa and Western Europe. Concomitantly, he is creatively active at a *chronological intersect* involving a fusion of traditional Arab and Berber narrative and various imported aesthetic impulses inspired by the work of modern poets around the world.

We believe that a close reading of the poems selected for *The Blueness of the Evening* can provide one with insight both into the work of one of Morocco's major contemporary poets and into the intermediating vectors of geographical, political, and linguistic ferment that have made Morocco an exciting hub of creative activity in the twenty-first century.

Eric Sellin and Mbarek Sryfi

ACKNOWLEDGMENTS

Some of the translations published here first appeared in bilingual presentation in a special Arabic double issue of *Metamorphoses* 19: 1/2 (Spring/Fall 2011).

We are grateful to Hassan Najmi for his permission to translate and publish his poems and for his assistance in clarifying several potential ambiguities.

I ▪ From *A Small Life*

Enemies

They shall know nothing about it.

You and I, alone—
and the clouds—
free.

But beware!
In our blood
there are embers under the ashes.

The Translator

Solitude with no satellite TV
and without the telephone ringing in the evening.
A solitude eliciting the wilderness of longing,
without another language.
We often mention the integrity of your words
         and the subtlety of your language.
But the translator is inured to proximities,
your feelings of doubt,
the police who practice the twisting of words,
. . . and you.

Cogito

I don't experience your doubts
and I say: *I am just like you—*
yet, I too know self-doubt.
Where will my steps lead me?
I doubt the very air I breathe.

Nor do I share your certainty.
And I say: *Like you, I pray to the wind.*

Sometimes

Sometimes the night seeks a place to call its own.
Sometimes the wind is late in arriving.
Sometimes the hand forgets it has fingers.
Sometimes the only thing one can do is rush toward the precipice.
Sometimes . . . I grow weary of this land.
Sometimes we just decide to do nothing all day.
Sometimes the flower looks for a face in the night.

Sometimes nothing remains but the thought of you.

Café Ibn Battuta

How am I to keep my hands busy on a sad evening! Blood in my
death-cup! Pigeons strut past the boundaries of fear. My legs
grow numb. Dogs on the periphery. Will any recollection of this
despair linger or must one capture this place with a sigh? In these
swelling shadows, is there anything for the fingers to do but help
one urinate. . . ? Between two clouds, above the railroad station,
the café sheds its shadow. The chairs have now been abandoned
by those who had been sitting there.

> Now I sit a little straighter.
> I think of my family.
> Meanwhile my friend is preparing the ink for
> > printing.
> I remember the ink being fenced in by phone
> > calls—
> the dream of revolution wrapped in advice.
> And now I recall my mother's voice:
> Beware of the raptors in the dark, my son!

> Should I be grateful for these clouds?

Point of View

What if, for a moment, you forgot time—
would it have reminded you of trembling ink?

What if you hadn't removed the curtains of cement—
would the view have then been complete?
What if you had forgotten that the curtains were there—
would the topography have come to *you*?

What if the wind were to remember its source—
would we then have even needed all this time?

The Warrior's Turn

I said I should sleep a while—
but this city fell heavily on my body.
How can I be free to embrace my silence?
When I am beset by all these wars,
am I to fight without hands?
In the evening, am I to keep pace with the failure of the stones
while following a strange itinerary?

The Poet

The poet who kept filling
his glass with poetry
couldn't keep on drinking
but continued to lean—
extinguishing his years in the ashtray.

Perhaps he could during his siesta. . . .
Perhaps he could gently rub his eyelids.

A Little Woman

She paused to cry in the rainy night,
weeping like the defenseless rain.
I did not raise my eyes from my book
nor did I wipe away her tears.

Before I lay down to sleep
she appeared in the last chapter of the novel.

In order not to cry
I closed the book, my head still on the pillow.

The Four Seasons

Roses arranged in a row
yet not exchanging a word.

These seasons move in rotation above me here where I lie.
They are neither talking with one another nor with me.

I lie here in silence—
conversing with each and every thing
but not with myself.

The Inn

At the neighborhood inn
I saw a shadow drinking a glass of wine.

And I am here,
feeling drunk.
And my words stagger.

Corrections

Tonight I will finish his image—
it would be better if he had straight hair and a scarred nose.
This mouth suits him without a tongue. And this
red may stir his blood. Tonight—

I teased him a bit and laughed at parts of his body. They needed
        to be
completed. I noticed his face—it was missing some small pieces.

I told myself, *Tonight I shall write him into existence*—
and soon his clay shall rise up under the sun of this
poem.

. . . .

. . . .

Now he has decayed—
he was dead even before the words had dried.

The Letters of Death

No water flowed under the bridge.
Heads straightened on shoulders.
The café is closed this morning, which is unusual.
The bakery is empty.
The bartender is drinking alone.

Clay

I can see my death.

—LEONARD NOLENS

I let the spewing gas devour the room's oxygen. I lay down to sleep as befits an enchanting death. I laugh when I remember how the worms of darkness will feed on the last illusions that bloat my body. I did not forget: There must be a curse fit for high status and me. I am not a criminal—
for I am returning this clay to its bed of clay.
. . . .

Now as I gaze up at the ceiling
I can touch my death with a glance.

The Musician

1

A remote silence nearing the shore of the soul.
(Does he know?)
It sings as though with a fleeting voice.
(How does he move all this air?)

2

The necks of the souls are laid on the altar of his *oud*—
his fingers move as though to breach the gates of hell.

3

These are his soul's movements resurrecting me—
and here I am offering him my body.

The Movie Critic

1

He looks at the mirror—
sipping his coffee as though in a scene from a movie.

2

In the crossing isthmus—
he fraternizes with the seen while hunting for the soul,
he vanishes in an evening of wisdom.

3

His continents are internal—
his eyeglasses shield his mind inside the skull.
He sees the picture in a flickering image.

4

His body is a light—
and he looks on with an impatient eye.

5

A man–mirror.
Glowing over there where the unknown occurs.

Together . . .

We sought refuge in the silence of the kiss. The candle, too, prepared our seclusion. We read poetry suitable for the silence. As though we were at the foot of a soul's cascade. We moved away from the door and the passing footsteps. We were lost in words for a moment (like anyone who loves life). I was smiling at her. She had opened her lips for me (maybe forever).

   I laughed—
   You sleep like a turkey! she said to me.
We took off our clothes to celebrate what remained of this fragility.

   Light is this shadow—
   at the onset of evening.

II ▪ From *The Bathers*

The Desert

For Muhammad Bahi: In Memoriam

*However, if the heart cannot hold up the hand in any
situation, then the arm cannot bear it either.*

—AL-MUTANABBI

1

Then I was suddenly overcome. *Where shall we ever find
a bit of shade in this
expanse of sand?* I asked him. Room for nothing
but reminiscences and loneliness.
A void. We were walking, surrounded by thorny plants.
The rocks had rusted. Thickets. And salt crust.
And dried riverbeds. The sand persisting in its dunes. So where does
this blinding glare come from?
Is it from this quartz or
from the granite rocks? His silence frightened me. I saw
lips crack and bleed and I saw the empty water jars.
My fears overwhelmed me. Are those dunes or the backs
of whales? Dunes or naked women?
I don't want your eyes to fade out; you have such a luminous soul.

2

He warned me about the sand. About the surface of the sand and
the sand hills. I had to pace myself for what

lay in store for us. Whenever I trusted a spot, the wind swept
the sand from under my feet. We kept on walking.
We are slowly giving up! I said. That vast
wild emptiness tears apart the soul. That entire mirage
is unattainable. And the land is dark. We walked night and day
and the distance stayed the same. We looked for oases only to find
dried-up marshes.

3

We arranged crowns of laurels on our heads.
We lit a fire and danced in the moonlight. United
in friendship. The guards had to be vigilant. We had to hold
rifles in our hands so the desert would not catch us by surprise,
                              unarmed.
I stared at the horizon with sleepy eyes: will they come
from here or from here or from over there?
As though we were fighting for our lives.

4

Flocks of sheep. The belligerent sun. And wolves. And the howling of
hyenas. Jackals. Lizards. Yet even full battle
gear wouldn't help. Nor the lions' manes on
the heads. Nor the scimitars.
Nor the shields. The dust clouds that hide all features. And the
                    . banners
that have become so dirty.
Among us were princes in their castles.
Among us were slaves in their rooms of clay
and straw.

And each of us was afraid for his reputation
as a warrior.
Then our camels scattered. And we collapsed. My comrades
          remained
by my side but they were as strangers. I walked among them
          without renouncing my distrust. And whenever I
          thought of continuing,
the idea came to me
to surrender.

5

Let me be quiet for a while, I said. I *talked
a lot. Don't worry,* he said, calming me. *Carry a handful of sand
          with you.
Put it in your pocket and touch it when the landscape
blurs or the compass fails.* And we sighed as
one. And whenever we understood, we resorted to silence
We would look away and hide our tears so that the craven
          cowards
would not be part of our defeat.
We would busy ourselves studying camel tracks.
He said we needed to check the camel droppings
to know where these invading camels had grazed. We were
astounded! Fraternal tribes . . . but some with no honor.
Allied, yet raiding one another. Someone would hand you
a rose and then kill you. You might find grass consolidated
in solitude but not a soul nearby.
Let's avoid talking for a while, I said to him.
Words are hell, he agreed.

6

No matter how fast we walked; no matter how slowly we walked;
we never arrived. Our steps were guided by fear. We got thirsty but
found no wells. We grew hungry but found no food. We would
throw
the sand in the air to convince those who didn't believe us. And
those who still don't. Oh, how many slopes and hollows we explored
without seeing anything. Oh. How we hoped. Oh, how we despaired.
Oh, how. . . .

7

Many were the times we woke at first light
but savored the warmth of the bed.
Many were the times we carried rifles on our shoulders but they
weren't loaded. Many were the times we fired bullets but missed
the birds or game. Many were the times we filled our gourds with
water, only to see it dry up along the way.
How many brothers we were who shared
in this brotherhood, yet I don't remember that we ever talked. So
much
silence and emptiness around us and our thoughts were not clear.

8

And because we were not accustomed to abbreviated signs,
we did not understand the camel driver.
He used to drive the camels at their own tempo,
at a lope, singing for us and for the road. But each one of us
has his own tune, his own tempo. We did not dread this path, as
such.
We dreaded it under these circumstances.

He taught me. The desert is not just a flat landscape.
No! Not just a wasteland of sand. And I came to know the
        desert.
It is all that space of loneliness within me.
I am a desert.
And now I am a desert within a desert.

9

Don't get upset. Protect your heart. It is better that
        perseverance
feed your soul. And with all these wounds. Stare
deeply into this sand so that its picture does not disappear
within you. You have a fistful of fresh hope. But your despair
is beautiful. You own all this light. But the sun disappears
at nightfall. How I wish I could keep up with you, but the hours
would lead me astray.
We were satisfied with a glimmer of light—you and I—
and with the waving of hands.
As if we were two beings in an elegiac poem.
Or as though I were to be left alone to remember you
when we die together.

10

We were together. He was chanting ancient poetry along the
        byways
of the night. As I listened to his accent within me, the flutes
chanted. And Al-Mutanabbi's insights overwhelmed me.
He was chanting and it was as though I were melting away.
He was chanting and it was as though
I were poised at the edge of a precipice. How could I not

hug him? Oh. . . ! I pronounce the opening verse and his
     memory
overflows. I recite, as does he. I remember him and he
     remembers me.
And the happiness. And the love. The poetry. And travel.
And the night. And the desert.
The spear. And the paper. And the pen. And it was as though we
had forgotten the last night we slept with our wives. As though
we had turned our backs on the sea and were now overwhelmed
by the land.
I placed my hand in his.
It scattered, as though I had grabbed a bunch of dried roses,
and we lost our way.

11

And when we returned to each other, you came to be . . .
like a sheep on the altar: decorated with sugar and dyed
with henna.
And since we were united by the thirst for extremes,
you suddenly grasped the handle of the earth's door
and left.

III ▪ From *Seclusion*

Condolences (I)

I know that you are sleeping at the source of life.
So I drink from the river's water—
in case it has passed by your body.

Condolences (II)

Caskets file by us every day.
We have begun to bury the Earth, which has grown old.

A Glance

I have been looking at you for two years—
yet my eyes have not become wrinkled.

Woman

A woman swam in cruelty,
extending her helping arms on the surface of the water.
Saving the sea from certain drowning.

Weeping

How did that happen between us?
I don't know. I closed my eyes and turned off the warning light.
A puff of air passed between us and I turned away to avoid
        seeing his face.
I dismissed him—
and I cried.

Message in a Bottle

I held the bottle to my mouth. I was trying to muffle my scream. At a remote beach I threw it in the rising water. I now know what will happen to that homeless bottle while I am in the Café Cupidon on the rue d'Algérie in Rabat. I know that pearl divers in a faraway gulf will hear my scream. I know that they have the amplifiers needed to read my message.

Cradle

Small cries.
I gesture with my hands.
Sparkles of color and light distract me.
And I absent-mindedly contemplate my eternity.

Dew

These are not dewdrops.
They are rather tears clinging to life—
they have lasted on the grass because of yesterday's leave-taking.

Chill

The sun hot on my arms.

And because you are here beside me—
I ponder the chill of the grass.

Scarf

The fluttering of your scarlet scarf makes the room tremble—
I realize that vines forsake their wine.

Seagull

Between sky and water, aloft in the blue.
Alone with your tears—

you have become a seagull whose nest is known to no one.

A Small Place

When he embraced her,
He spurned the rest of the world.
And he was satisfied with this small place—
in her arms.

Stones

Lonely stones
eroded by solitude.
The sound of a flute comes to them from far away.
They are not moved.
Flashes of light pass them.
The stones see them as fires in the making.

Voice

Alone in the room—
I make my ears listen to my last poem.

I become frightened by my own words.

Dyads

In the night of your eyes
no light shall guide me but that of your body.

What step shall I choose for our dance
while all my body's music is muted?

Why waste time on words?
And how do I rid my body of the silence?

Everything would disappear within me were I to disappear.
Nothing remains after my body's disappearance.
Except it: my body.

The Blueness of the Evening

I yearn for other places where I can see you.
Grass where we might relax.
A thirsty tongue for drinking and to call your name.
I yearn for the night.
I yearn for other doubts to fill my days
and I yearn for you.

In the blueness of the evening, how I yearn
and how I don't—

Oh! The trembling that comes with the cloud cover of night!

N. A.

An evening on the brink of your night,
like an afternoon fading with the last notes of sunshine . . .
inexorably.
As though you had no body.
Time trembles at the edge of your soul,
as though you were to awaken light itself from its nap.

At night
you strip the sky of its stars.

The Station Square

A female tourist at the train station. A newspaper and tobacco kiosk. A sad newspaper. At the bottom of its page, a small box for forgetting. Hands holding burnt-out cigarettes. Angry swollen veins. Clouded faces. A closed bar. Police everywhere in the headlines. Police ruining the cities. A crime in the park. Police videos of half bodies. Two lovers on the right-hand sidewalk. Bare legs. A maid emptying a bucket of water in the entryway. A doorman dozing by the entrance to a building. An advertisement on the gate of the institute. Leftover leaflets on the ground. A curtainless window. An evening of anger. Anger sneaks home to the television sets. TV programs on health awareness. A sermon. A chat in front of the post office. A woman complaining about the woman next door. A little girl in pajamas standing by the window. A ghost walks to his bed. A muddy newspaper clipping. Vigilance among friends. Solidarity of nature. Fallen sentiments. Expressions of admiration. Speeches full of hyperbole. Bribery. Time differences. Immunity from immunity. Endless distortions. Silence emanating from our pores. Dead cities. Cities. Cemeteries. . . .

My glass and I—
dodging the shadows at the Café Ibn Battuta.
Where are you? Why have you not come?

Heavy is the night in my body!

Dyad

Two bodies embrace.

From which of your heart's windows will you be looking at me?
I, like a moon behind the clouds, whisper to you.
How do I reach you?

> *You need not hurry!*
> *My body is torn asunder.*
> *And I am intoxicated with you—*
How would you rest on my lawn?

Just let me lose my way.

The Empty Chair

In the evening. Every evening I walk solemnly toward the empty beach. Only the water is there. Only the sand. And the sun has turned pale. It appears to be stationed there upon the declining horizon. I have placed two chairs on the pebbles and on the sand that the tide hardened a while before. I wait for you to come and sit here before me so we might speak a moment about the body. About the water when it grows lonely (*Joliment seule!*). About the solitude of the view. About the meaning of death. About friends who usually scatter right after a burial ceremony. And about the distant sky. About the hole in the ozone layer. About everything—

but you don't have faith in the mermaids.

You prefer to gaze at the view of the empty chair on the empty
       beach.

That's why you won't come out of the drowning water that
       desired your flesh.

You insist that the color of mourning be blue.

The sun has assumed the shape of an orange on the plate of the
       sunset.

It is my sole witness.

IV ▪ *Umber Winds*

Umber Winds

I

Date palms stripped bare—
and arid is the infinite landscape in your eyes.

Suddenly all the oases are clouded with the filth of banners.

~

The luckiest rose—
the shadow of the bombing in the night protected it.

~

The grass in search of sunlight.
The stone waiting for the night.

Both evoke tears.

~

Umber Winds may be read as a long poem and/or as a suite of
short haiku-like poetic images. The poems, published in 2005 by
Editions Marsam in Rabat, were first conceived in the early 1990s as
a collaborative project that juxtaposed Najmi's texts and a series of
black-and-white ink washes by Moroccan artist Mohamed Kacimi
in a joint response to the massive aerial bombardment of Baghdad
in January and February of 1991.—Trans.

The hills with no name
provide shelter for a death lurking
under the sands of time.

~

We've had enough of mourning.
Let us now shed mercy
on the shattered dead stones.

~

On the pillow of the wind . . .
we sniffed the scent of death hidden in the grass.

Rustlings of rising haze,
proclaiming the awakening of the blood that remains.

~

The river that left the bridges in a shambles
proceeded—crystal clear—towards the bed of its repose.

~

Bridge spans fall into the river
but the bridges of words never collapse.

And the water proudly moves forward to its throne.

~

Leave the river of blood now.
There is a dew in the eyes
that will never dry.

You can see it—
and the eye is jealous of its own tears.

~

Ah!
I saw the defenseless open window overlooking the river,
bleeding . . .
late at night.

~

. . . .

The bridge is fortunate enough—
half of it collapsed into the water.

The bridge!

~

Have you visited the broken bridge?
The bridge—

Oh, it still harbors so many glorious days for the days to come!
Oh, it still harbors so much blood for the blood!

II

Leave the windows open.
The invisible airplanes won't be coming, tonight

we shall be bombarded by our old wounds.

~

The night of war found no respite.
Frightened, it remained awake with us in the children's room.

~

Here I await the dead . . .
and polish the array of copper plaques on the wall.

From Babel to my body,
a single blood fraternizes with death
and dusts off the relics of the soul.

~

A mother stands by the oriel window.
She is watching over the public square—

perhaps the statue will lose a hand of marble or brass.

~

Seen from the windows the moon appears sad.
All the rooms have fallen asleep
with neither bread nor water.

After a few moments,
a cloud moves by
heavily armed with aircraft.

~

The airplanes come hunting the moon
and death's meteors rain down on the empty roofs.
Tonight there is no window

permitting one Arab to see another!

~

We had turned out the light in the room.
And we had opened our lips to drink from the glass of kisses.
And the attacking airplanes had come
and I found no mouth near mine.

Martyred were the kisses, and the sky
had been commandeered for the bombings.

~

Closed doors.
Ash-covered windows.
And fragments of the bombs left on scorched stones.

Is that why the streets are desolate . . .
and why the feet are wary of the sidewalk's cleanness?

~

In the darkened room I was wrapped
in the atmosphere of the place.

And outside my body . . .
outside the walls—
Monday slipped by in sadness.

~

Record your wounds in the fireplace of time.

The document does not forget.
Perhaps the soul will make the erasures.

III

A land for the orphaned—
the writing's sky is lush
with the foliage of shrapnel.

~

Piles and piles!
Do all these papers cause anxieties?
Airplanes between the lines . . . and armor-clad words.

War!

~

Armies in hot places
putting the soul's ice on the steel helmets.

~

"Ah, ils vont encore venir. . . !"

Breton,
why do you call for help, Oh crazy poet?
This weapon has the multi-hued hair of all the continents.

And I have plenty of blood to spare.

〜

The glass of tea grew cold.
The sentry grew cold under a gray sky.

Only death's red button is hot.
And the sun.
And the memory of the light ablaze with its hue.

〜

The bombs signed by the general
were slow to reach us.
We were able to read death's alphabet . . .
but we could not make out the signature.

Death was mocking us—
as would a deep well.

〜

Who will keep company with the orphaned glass
when all the drunks have headed for the bridges of death?

On their chests
tons of explosives shall wake!

~

Cheeks of clay—
tears shed upon the ground

as though falling from a faraway sky.

~

Soon the clouds of iron shall weave a veil for the moon.

—*Can you point out the way to the blood bank?*

~

Have the invisible planes come to wipe out this place?
Tell me! But—

where shall time land?

~

The hands of the clock have forgotten their daily duties.

Thank God for my heart's steady beat.
It is still alive.

~

He . . .
collects the nights in the closet
and covers heads with palm fronds of light

so that the memories will not abandon him.

Oh, how he loves his wounds
to raise high his blood.

~

Country as memory.
A country where the wine sings (said Éluard)

Take up your glass . . .
and drink the nectar of the soul.

IV

Why have you lowered your head
like the wax of a half-spent candle?
Raise high your despair, Oh Brother! Your despair!

~

The red flees my memory
and the black comes from the neighboring sky.

We are seeking a name for the gray . . .
and we find only words riddled with terror.

~

The face whose eyes I loved
will not remain the same

and I, too, shall make some changes.

~

—Laugh. . . .
—And what is left of one's lips?
. . . .

. . . .

Even in this destruction, try to find the stone of memory
so as not to doze away what is left of time . . .
and of clay.

~

. . . .

And the vacant eyes—
what do they see that can make the world notice the stones'
            pain?

My horizon is injured and I shall treat it with my wounds.
I have two eyes
and I shall not stuff them in the pocket of defeat.

~

And you. . . .
Our love for you smoothed our wrinkles.
May your name wipe the lips
of every talkative mouth.

Beautiful is the dew in your eyes.
And no one helps the rose shed tears.

~

Clean off the benches in the parks
that the martyrs might rest there.

There is no need for caskets.

~

And you. . . .
On account of your eyes,
I shall not abandon my body.

~

But I forgot to mention:
When the bombing began near a pile of stones
I left to go sleep

On the other bank of the night.

V ▪ From *A Hurt like Love*

A Tear

He never used to cry. He never even thought of crying. But a tear caught him unawares. As though it were late for an appointment. As though it hadn't made it in time for the old crying. As though it were racing to overtake the old crying. As though it were not a tear!

The Runaway's Nostalgia

In Rabat. In the house. At night alone— I, the runaway, am trying to see. . . .

I can't stop the aroma of grilled meat coming from afar or that of baked bread coming from my language. Whenever I try to get hold of you, I find my father's image competing with this onrush of memories. Whenever I try to acknowledge love, I find my mother sitting, selling bread. Here I am alone, my head a bustling countryside market. I see my mother's picture and I see the bread stand. I hear my father's voice and the grilling fumes rise out of my head. The butchers' voices swarm over me. The bleating of sheep being led to slaughter reaches me. And I see country folks going back and forth in the square between the vegetables and used shoes and clothes. Between meat, bread, and oil . . . and the gendarmes.

This soft faraway noise always gets closer. This reminiscence that punishes forgetfulness. And this joy brightens my face. Like the face of a dead person without consolation.

The face of a dead person who did not deserve to die. Like the face of an abandoned dead person.
In Rabat. Like a faraway wind breaking my windpipe.
At night. Like a sleepy sun coming to erase half the shade near me.
I give her my name so that the day starts at night.
And because my name is not for anyone
I say: Why don't I abandon it to hell?

A Man Contemplating His Life

I am empty and dark like an oven.

Poèmes épars—MAX JACOB

Light from bare balconies.
Maybe they continue to stay awake or to court late at night.
I see colors on the clothesline,
dark . . .
there on the neighbors' roofs,
and the Moroccan gardener is washing up in the embassy
      courtyard.
Standing looking out from the balcony as at an oil painting,
I am suspicious of the clouds rapidly crossing a shimmering sky.
I see the government workers cleaning the streets.
Above their heads hang banners that lazy organizers had
      forgotten to remove.
The last scavenger parks his car.
He pokes his head in the trashcans along the empty street.
Stray dogs flirt with a confused female cur in the night.
On a passing truck horses hug with their necks,
as if headed to the slaughterhouse.
A drunken driver almost flips over at the curve.
The windows, still awake, are startled by the brakes.
I turn to look at your gaze.
There is tedium between us.
I open my eyes wide, contemplating the radiance of your face.

As if I saw it falling on the other side.
Like a chord that has lost its yearning for the tune,
I stand here waiting for someone or something.
I put my hand on the cold wood at night.
I have become submissive to the night as though my soul didn't
resemble me anymore.
I stand here on the balcony—
contemplating my life.

Voices in the City

Don't trust what you see.

—C. P. CAVAFY

Evening. In the capital.
The wall I see through the window in front of me seems to
　　　grow darker.
(The scene of a wall becoming darker in an old prison.)
The sound of windows being closed in the building.
(They locked the cells a little while ago. The sound of the steel
　　　door.)
This is the best of Rabat,
when the night comes early!
(The best of the prison is to withdraw from the world and the
　　　people.)
There is nothing that scares us here.
All evil is with us behind doors.
Prisoners are here.
Free people are here.
And us—
we, whose patience has rotted inside us.
With half a tongue (we speak).
With half a heart (we love).
With half a lung.
With half the effort.
We, who hurt our throats.

Our voices are becoming low.

We have a hoarseness like that of drunken singing.

We save what is left of our breath.

We sing all night long.

Early in the morning,

we are let out to get some sun in the prison yard.

Then, after the wall has become darker,

we resume singing.

No one hears half voices.

There in the cell of the old prison. Here in the capital.

The Violins

While in jail awaiting execution, Socrates heard
a musician sing a poem by the Sicilian poet
Stesichorus (sixth century, BCE), and he begged him
to teach him the song. When the singer asked about
the need for a song, Socrates replied:
"I have to learn it before I die."

— *XXXVIII*, 4 , AMMIANUS MARCELLINUS

I am from over there.

The wind brings the sounds of violins.

I sing the song of my old love.

As if I had a violin held on my knee.

The horses are present in the song.

Nothing except blankets and bed sheets

(white and cold).

No one with me except the memory of your voice.

Sing for me your way.

Sing for me what no listener requests.

I will hear you even from afar . . . even from beyond the dirt.

I repeat the words we sang together.

I float over your voice.

I take off my hat and bow in respect or with apologies to the road,

as I walk in the distance alone.

Oh . . . how I wish the violinist were a bit more gentle on the violin.

Its bow is not meant for butchering.

The Rain in the Poem

It is raining cats and dogs
in the poem.
The wind is blowing.
Storms and lightning.
Walls collapse.
Roofs and carts drift by on the water.
Children are playing,
leaping over the storm drains.
The tumult of passers-by.
The zinging of bullets.
The slamming of steel gates.
Blood flowing on the sidewalk.
All of that is in the poem.
And I don't hear anything; I don't hear anyone;
I don't see anything.

Whispers

My words were naked when I chanced upon them.
They were exchanging whispers of love,
arousing their starved emotions.
The purity of shyness upon their letters.
As if they had flung aside their covering to appear on the earth.
As if they had a taste of cloves on their tongues.
As if.

And even without hearing a thing
I was aware of everything.

A Cloud

We were worried about his silence.
Never a word.
We exhausted him with our questions,
with our stares,
and with our repeated winks.
Perhaps he grew tired of us,
tired of the vacuum surrounding him,
of a deceitful light he used to be promised.
Then he turned his head away
and strode off towards the cloud.
We watched his progress
in silence,
watching from behind his back.
Before his shadow disappeared,
he waved to us—
and then, right there, he became a cloud.

Sands

My sands quietly bask in the sun.
Their silence is lonely.

This sea tyrannizes them with every tide.

A Room in Rome

In Rome, in the Via Salaria,
in the Hotel Panama Garden,
I preferred that the room remain shrouded in darkness.
I preferred to remain alone,
no other breaths mixing with mine,
without attractive lighting in the room and no lamp on,
with only the bitter feelings worthy of a poem.
I don't care about the passing of time nor the crowds of people.

Alone. Without light. Without gloomy half-spent candles.
I say to my darkened room: I place my trust in the darkness.

Love

I had a childhood which I then forgot.
I remembered my first milk on your chest.
I began to love the insomnia of your breast.
To dart about and migrate to your nest like a sparrow.

I began to seek the sanctuary of another language—
to say I love you.

In the Darkened Room

You flung yourself on the bed, full of desire.
Your secret warmth slipped into my veins.
Into my body slipped the fire of your body.

In the late-night quietude,
let me see you with my fingers.
There is light enough in my heart.
Enough yearnings for fulfillment.

Escape

I cover my pain with pictures and put my sadness into words.
I look inattentively as though to let my eyes betray my love.
She is here beside me; she wants me to whisper something to
       her—
and I have nothing to say.
I have begun to prefer this silence in this shadow
and when I wet her with kisses,
I murmur what a stranger tells a stranger,
as if my words were filled with water.

. . . .

Oh, whoever hears the voice of a man drowning alone
is swept away by a muddy river and together they plunge into
       an ebbing sea.

The Dead Man

A hand too cold to belong to this world.
—PHILIPPE JACCOTTET

His clothes were hanging behind the door. They were there for
    two months.
He had not worn the clothes in his closet for months. There
    were suits discarded years ago. As if he used to go
    out naked.
As if he were dead and, to hold on to his memory, his family
    had never emptied his closet.

The Poet (II)

He said he saw people made of glass going by.
His daughter looked out but did not see anyone passing.
She woke him up—
she dreaded that the poem's sleepwalking would take him away.
She dreaded that he would be one of them . . .
and that he would shatter.

Borges I

Your night is deeper than the night.
My eyes are like yours.
. . . .

How beautiful is this blindness that accompanies us.
Together we are what we do not see.

Borges II

When you stand up to leave, the entire earth stands up to follow in your footsteps. As if your share of your ancestors' bodies were following you. You have the blessing of the road. You have a walking stick that invents the distance for you. As if the wind were to part, left and right, so that your sight might cross. Even though you are sightless, without eyes. Blind like I am. Except that I doubt that you do not see. I doubt it.

I Change the Universe Just a Bit

I am ablaze, as if there were a fire inside me.
I stretch out my left arm to girdle your waist.
My hand moves down to the thicket of the shadow.
I see you high up and I leap to reach the top foliage as a deer
    would.
As if the shadow of the kiss were to remove the redness of the
    scarf from your cheek.
I hurry. I hurry to claim you as mine.
I sway on the clouds that have cracked under me.
I am elated.
The wind carries me off.
The wings and the breeze. The scepter. The face.
The neck. The chest. All belong to me.
The belly. The waist. The touch. The kiss. And the privilege.
And the queen's goblet to drink from.
And the flame.

I am shaken by longing now.
The stripes on the tigress's fur have tempted the deer.
I am being shattered. My organs are falling apart.
My emotions mingle with yours.
I am changing the universe just a bit.